Small Business Planning Made Simple

What To Consider Before You Invest

Lisa Woods

ISBN-10: 1544266529
ISBN-13: 978-1544266527

INTRODUCTION

Owning a small business is a dream for many of us. Whether it happens organically from a hobby, or strategically via personal & outside investment - making a business successful *over time* requires planning.

Dreaming Big is an important step in the process; it's what motivates entrepreneurs. Dreaming defines the business idea. It inspires us, it inspires others, and often *distracts* entrepreneurs from taking realistic steps toward a profitable functioning business. That's where Small Business Planning comes in.

Small Business Planning is all about cultivating the startup process and determining the long-term feasibility of your dream.

This book is designed to take your dream through the startup and feasibility process: Think through the risks, align the tools & structure, define practical steps, and calculate realistic rewards before making your decision to invest.

If you are ready to take your great idea to the next level, this book will guide you through that process. More than just a template, **it explains in simple terms** what you need to think through, how to go about it, why the information is important and how to use it properly.

The ultimate goal of your Small Business Plan is not to impress someone with words on a template, it's to empower you, with a realistic roadmap & timeline to evaluate the potential success of your dream; an essential stepping-stone to making it a reality.

HOW TO USE THIS BOOK

Chapters 1-15 of this book will guide you through the step-by-step process of writing a business plan.

Chapter 16 provides some great tips that you can use to improve the effectiveness of your plan.

Chapter 17 is a blank template for taking notes right here in the book so that you can start building the framework for your business as you go.

By the time you get done reading and writing in this book, you will be prepared to construct an honest and productive plan for your small business to implement.

CONTENTS

1

GENERAL BUSINESS INFORMATION

This first section of your business plan is meant to define basic information about you, your business and how you got to this point in the first place.

Here's what you need to define:

Primary Ownership & Status

- Who will officially own the business?
- What % of ownership will each owner have (if multiple owners)?
- What type of legal entity have you created, or do you plan to create (Sole Proprietorship/LLC/Partnership/Other)?
- What is, or will be, the physical location (address) of the business?
- What is the phone #/email/fax (if already set up)?
- What is the address for your Website/Twitter/Facebook/Other Social Media you have or plan to set up?

Experience

What relevant experience do you have in the type of business you are creating?

Company Name

What are you going to call the business?

Why Are You Interested In This Business?

What is it about this specific business that appeals to you? What is your intent for the business? Is it to expand a hobby for some extra income, or to provide financial independence to fully support yourself and your family?

How Did You Come Up With The Idea?

What was the trigger that sparked and advanced the concept of your new business?

Industry Description

How would you describe the "sector" your business is part of?

For example: If you make pens or pencils, your industry would be "Writing Instrument Manufacturers". If you make necklaces, your industry would be "Custom Jewelry Producers". If you are providing home inspections, your industry would be the "Home Inspection Industry". If you are building patios, you may be part of the "Home Contractor Industry", the "Landscaping Industry" or "Pool & Patio Design Contractors".

Industry is defined by a collective group of companies that are similar to yours. It's important to define this properly so you can research and understand your competitors, as well as learn from them: their products, their strengths and upcoming trends. You might even find a useful industry association to join and participate in.

Monthly Revenue "Today"

If you already have a business that you are looking to expand upon or diversify, it's important to define your current revenue stream per month and over the course of the past year.

If your new business is starting from zero activity before it, that's OK too, you would state that case in this section.

Products & Services

What products and/or services is your business currently offering (if an existing business)? What new products and/or services is your business planning to offer as a result of this business plan? Please describe each specific product or service in as much detail as possible.

Target Revenue In 24 Months

Below is an example:
Year 0: $18,000 ($1.5k/average month)
Year 1: $48,000 ($4k/average month)
Year 2: $71,000 ($5.9k/average month)

Year zero means the last 12 months of business if your business has been active in some form prior to the launch of this new business plan. Year one is the plan for the first 12 months going forward and year two is the revenue plan for months 13-24.

The reason we refer to "12 month periods" instead of "calendar years" such as 2018, 2019, etc., is because you may start your business in a month other than January. Planning based on a *length of time* vs. a *fixed year*, is a more realistic view to target and track your success at startup. If year zero was less than 12 months, just state that as a side note with the number of months that made up the year. For example: **Year 0**: $18,000 ($2.5k/average month over a 7 month period)

Current Business Status

What has been done so far to implement your business plan, and what is currently in the works? For example: Have your set up your LLC? Reserved your website address? In discussions with investors? Built/building inventory for the launch?

What Will The Largest Revenue Generator Be For Your Business?

Go back to the list of products and services you listed for your business and break down the Year One sales for each product. You can itemize year two as well if there is a change in the primary sales generator. Below is an example of a *Candle & Soap* company:

Soy Candles: Year 1 Estimate $28,800 (60% of total sales)
Bath Salts: Year 1 Estimate $14,400 (30% of total sales)
Soaps: Year 1 Estimate $4,800 (10% of total sales)

The month-by-month ramp-up detail will be shown on your financials later on in the plan. At this point you can just estimate them, then come back and modify later. Make sure your detailed financial plan matches this section once your business plan is complete!

What Part of Your Business Is Not Easily Found In Other Businesses?

Referring back to your "Industry Description", what does your business have that sets you apart from most of your competitors? Maybe it's a special service you offer that is not common in the industry, unique delivery terms, make to order vs. limited stock items. Or maybe you have a location where competitors simply don't exist.

It's possible this part of your business can be copied, but today, you know that it is not commonplace.

What Part of Your Business Cannot Be Replaced By A Competitor?

Referring once again back to your "Industry Description", what is it about your business that is totally yours? Something that competitors in your industry don't have or can't have because it is uniquely you. Maybe it's a secret formula, a patent, or unique relationships based on your background.

Take some time to define this and think about the value it will bring to your business. Try to quantify that value by putting the benefit into words that you can then use to market & price your product effectively.

What Part Of Your Business Cannot Be Duplicated Without Significant Investment?

This question is about financial barriers to entry. If someone wanted to copy your business to the best of their ability, not an exact copy, but close enough to get into the industry, what significant financial hurdles would they need to overcome in order to start it up? Would they need a storefront, or can they use a home office? Would they need to invest in dump trucks, or use their minivan? Are there insurance costs, or significant licensing fees required?

How about a specific educational requirement that takes time and money to achieve?

These barriers are important to understand so that you (and any potential investors) have an awareness of the ease at which new competition can come in and take market share from you. If your business plan is strong and the financial barriers to entry are high, that's a low risk investment. But if your plan is just OK, and it's really easy to get into this business, that makes it much more risky to investment money into your idea. It's a balance, and that's why developing a robust business plan is much more than filling out a template. Each component of your plan should tie together to tell a confident story, with clear actions that make it real.

2

BUSINESS & FINANCIAL OBJECTIVES

This section of your business plan is meant to define the financial investment required to start up or expand the business, the sales estimates and growth patterns over the course of the business plan, as well as the break even point for the business (how long it will take to make a profit).

Here's what you need to define:

Startup/Investment & Other Capital Requirements

This is where you build the list of items you need to purchase in order to move forward. Line item by line item, what do you need and how much will each item cost?

We recommend you think through multiple options such as new equipment vs. used equipment, and outline the pros and cons of each. You might even put a timeline on investment choices. For example, you have startup equipment for one product/service launch, and then once you achieve a minimum revenue goal, the second phase of investment takes place.

You always want to spend the least amount of money necessary upfront, so that the business can fund investment as it grows. The tendency however, is to get as much as possible done upfront for a perfect start. In practice you will find that assumptions change once the business is in motion; it's better to take it step by step, than re-spend on investments that you made assumptions on too soon. This is a sound philosophy when investing your own cash, as well as applying for a loan. If you can show a sequential investment plan aligned with targeted results…and then achieve those results, everyone will feel more confident investing in your future.

Projected Rate Of Return On Investment

In simple terms, the projected rate of return is the speed at which your business should start to make a real profit. This cannot be calculated without building your financial plan (Chapter 14 of this book), but once have your financial plan completed, you will carry that detail over to this section to define how long it will take to earn your investment back. Then you can make a decision if you are OK with that timeline.

Your financial plan should consist of yearly sales revenue, less any raw material costs (COGS), operating costs (marketing, utilities, rent, supplies, loan payments, payroll, etc.), and taxes. What you are left with is your profit.

Next is an example of how your projected rate of return would be calculated:

Initial Investment: $15,000.00

	Year 1	Year 2	Year 3
Sales Revenue	**$48,000**	**$57,600**	**$63,360**
COGS	($18,000)	($21,375)	($23,760)
Operating Costs	($25,000)	($25,000)	($25,000)
Taxes	($1,400)	($3,143)	($4,088)
Profit	**$3,600**	**$8,082**	**$10,512**

Your rate of return is calculated by simply adding up how long it will take to earn back your investment. In this case YR1 earned $3,600 in profit and YR2 $8,082 in profit totaling $11,682. At the end of YR2 you still have not earned back your initial investment of $15,000. The plan states that YR3 will earn $10,512 in profit. If you divide YR3 by 12 months, that equates to $876 per month ($10,512/12=$876.00). Next you need to figure out how many months in year three are needed to make up the difference. See below:

Initial Investment:		**($15,000)**
YR1 Profit over 12 months	+$ 3,600	
		($11,400) left to pay off
YR2 Profit over 12 months	+$8,082	
		($ 3,381) left to pay off
YR3 Profit over 4 months	+$3,504	
		$ 123 actual new money!

In the above example it will take 2 years and 4 months to pay off the initial investment and start making new money (real profit).

Once you have this calculation, you are better able to assess if the timeframe is acceptable to you. There is no black or white answer to this question.

Obviously if the reason you are interested in this investment is to be financially independent and fully support yourself and your family with the income, then you need to make sure you can support yourself by other means until the business makes enough money per year to achieve that goal.

The other question you need to ask is…are these financial projections realistic? Will it take longer to get customers to buy your product or service? Should the ramp-up of sales be spread out a little further? A good way address this is to create two separate financial scenarios. Assume your first scenario is an "aggressive" one. Now create a second set of financial assumptions with a longer first year ramp up. This is considered to be your "conservative" estimate. Calculate your return on investment for each scenario. You now have better information for determining your risk. Can you accept this risk? If not, what can you do to improve the security (likelihood of success) of your plan?

Each component of your business plan has an impact on your likelihood of success. The more detailed the components of the plan are, the greater likelihood they will be implemented, and the greater visibility you will have to tweak things once you get started.

Now that you have an indication of how long it will take to make "new money", let's take a look at another important success indicator, your breakeven point, which determines how much you need to sell each month in order to make a profit. It starts with understanding your operating and payroll expenses.

Estimated Operating Costs & Payroll

This section is pulled from your income statement (Chapter 14). Here you will present a summary of where your business spends money. For example, using the income statement provided in Chapter 14 for the *Candle & Soap Company*, the Operating & Payroll Cost Summary is as follows:

	Year 1	**Year 2**
Operating Expenses	$23,150	$13,550
Payroll	$ 0	$ 0
Total Expenses	**$23,150**	**$13,550**

It's important to look at each year of your plan because YR1 includes some startup costs that don't exist in year two. A summary explanation would be helpful. For example:

- 100% of business expenses are operational. No employee hires are considered in the plan period.
- YR1 Operating costs include $9,400 of startup costs for the website launch. This is considered a variable cost since it is a one-time expense. Therefore YR2 is a better representation of fixed (ongoing) expenses.

Estimated Breakeven & Profitability Points

The breakeven point tells you the minimum amount of sales revenue your business must achieve in order to cover its costs each month, and in total for the year. The profitability point is really, by definition, similar to the breakeven point, however conceptually this is the point at which your business must reach before it can start making a profit. Therefore any sales dollars achieved over the breakeven point, are pure profit that you can put in the bank. Those sales are not going to be used to pay any business costs because costs have already been taken out of the revenue generated before you got to that point.

The calculation is the following: Total Fixed Operating & Payroll Expenses divided by Sales Gross Margin %. Here's how to calculate your breakeven & profitability points using the *Candle & Soap Company* example. There are four steps.

1) Calculate Your Fixed Operating & Payroll Expenses

	Year 1	**Year 2**
Operating Expenses	$23,150	$13,550
- Variable Expenses	($9,400)	($ 0)
+ Payroll	$ 0	$ 0
Total Fixed Expenses	**$13,750**	**$13,550**

* The variable expenses were defined in the operating costs as one-time website startup expenses. Fixed expenses are costs that are incurred each month.

2) Calculate Your Sales Gross Margin %

	Year 1	**Year 2**
Revenue	$44,633	$77,063
- COGS	($20,460)	($35,907)
Gross Income	$24,173	$41,156
Gross Margin %	**54%**	**53%**

* GM% is calculated by (GM% / Revenue)

3) Calculate Your Breakeven Point Per Year

	Year 1	Year 2
Total Fixed Expenses	$13,750	$13,550
/ GM%	54%	53%
Breakeven Point (Year)	**$25,463**	**$25,566**

* Breakeven Point Per Year is calculated by (Total Fixes Expenses / GM%)

4) Breakeven Point Per Month

	Year 1	Year 2
Breakeven Point Per Year	$25,463	$25,566
/ Months In Year	12	12
Breakeven Point (Month)	**$ 2,122**	**$ 2,130**

* Breakeven Point Per Month is calculated by (Breakeven Point per year / # of months in year)

Now let's look at how to use this information. In the *Candle and Soap Company* example we can look at our revenue projection and see that we will achieve our breakeven point during YR1, month seven. Once we reach that point, we know the business should be making a profit baring any variable costs or investments that may take place. Seven months to build a viable, profitable business - that's not so bad!

If you look at the income statement you'll find it shows a profit of $721 during the month of May (month 5). In this example, the difference between using the raw data from your income statement and using the estimated breakeven indicator is only two months. The reality (if everything in your plan comes to fruition) will probable be a profit between 5 to 7 months of starting your business.

Ask yourself the question – can you support yourself and your business expenses with other funds until that breakeven and profit point is achieved? If the answer is yes, that's great news. If the answer is no, then you need to go back through your plan and try to reduce costs or ramp up the business at a more reasonable pace.

Once again, there is no "correct" answer when it comes to breakeven and profitability points. These are just indications that allow you to validate your business concept and determine if you can, and want to, move foreword with your investment of time and money.

3

BUSINESS SYSTEMS

This section of your business plan details the tools you will use to manage the day-to-day operation. A system can be as simple as a pre-printed notebook, an excel spreadsheet, or as complex as industry specific software that can be used to create a competitive advantage. The point is to define what your business will use so those costs (if any) can be incorporated into your plan. If a specific system requirement does not apply to you, just be clear on that point. For example, if you don't plan on having employees, you wont need a payroll system to manage them!

Here is what you need to define:

Order Management & Processing Systems

What system will you use to take orders for products or services, manage those transactions throughout the processing cycle until the product or service has been delivered?

Accounting System

What system will you use manage your books (payables, receivables, taxes)?

Purchasing System

What system will you use to manage your inventory, your suppliers & order levels?

Payroll System

What system will you use to track employee working hours & vacations, as well as process payroll checks?

Project Management & Production Systems

What system will you use manage any large projects, or your overall production process/planning.

Product/Service Delivery & Quality Control

What system will you use to track delivery times, customer feedback, quality issues, and manage consistent quality levels?

Client Acquisition & Maintenance

What system will you use to maintain customer information (order history, contacts, sales follow-up, quotations)?

System Evolution

Will your systems need to advance over the next 12 to 24 months as your business develops? If so, how?

4

OPERATING COSTS & ORGANIZATIONAL STRUCTURE

This section of your business plan defines who will be responsible for each job in your company, as well as how your operating costs will be structured.

Here is what you need to define:

Principles: Management Expertise & Relevance to the Business

Describe the management or business experience of each business owner, as well as how that experience will specifically benefit the success of the company.

There is a big difference between doing the work and managing the business. This section is an opportunity to think through the support you need to compensate for any experience shortfalls that exist.

In-House Services VS Outsourced

Describe what work will be conducted by you and your team, as well as any work that is done by an outside service. Some examples of outside services include payroll, accounting, and partnerships with other companies or suppliers.

Responsibility Matrix

Who will be doing each job within your company? The answer can be as simple as "I'm going to do everything", or as detailed as creating a full-blown organizational chart.

If you have more than a sole proprietor in the business, we highly recommend that you detail a division of responsibilities. Who is going to do what, and who will have the final decision power over each area of responsibility? By defining this upfront you will set your business up for a smoother existence. One of the biggest stumbling blocks in any company, big or small, is communication of roles & responsibilities: Who is going to do what? Who works for whom? Who will make decisions? Who will be held accountable for what?

By defining this in an org chart you not only answer those questions, but you can define the gaps as well. Gaps are required jobs that the business needs to function, even though at this point you may not have, or be able to afford, anyone qualified to fill them. As a small business owner you are bound to wear many hats and fill those roles yourself…for now. Defining roles will ensure they are on your radar so important functions do not fall through the cracks. Below is an example of an organizational chart for a *Consulting Business* startup:

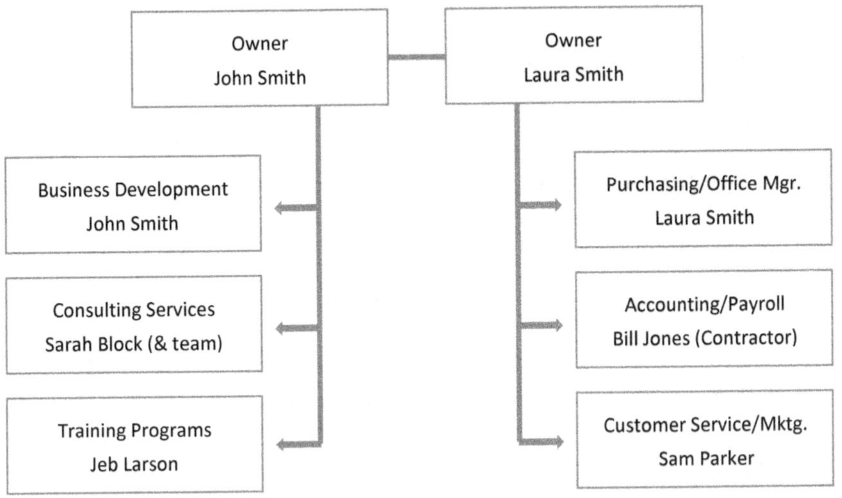

Access to Labor Over Ramp-Up Period

As you start your business, as well as during the time it may expand…how easy or difficult will it be to hire qualified people to fill jobs in your company? Are there special skills, qualifications or experience requirements for your business? Is the local labor pool easy to access or will it be difficult to find employees?

Office/Operating Space Requirement & Plan

Where will the business reside? Is it in your home? If so, how much square footage will be used? Will you need a separate phone line? Internet hookup? Do you need to modify the space at all to get started?

Do you own land where the business will be located? If you need to rent or purchase space, where will it be? How much and what kind of space will you need? How much will it cost?

Once you've outlined your startup environment, how will your space need to adapt over time? Do you plan to expand? What milestones need to be met in order to implement that expansion plan?

Patents, Insurance, Legal Requirements/Permits & Licenses

What special requirements apply to your business? Do you have an invention that requires a patent? Does your industry require specific liability insurance due to high risk services or products? Do you need to obtain any special permits or licenses to startup or maintain your business?

Each of these requirements bares a cost that should be incorporated into your plan. They may also have a timeframe associated with achieving them. The good news is that these special requirements become barriers to entry for potential competitors.

Payment Expectations for Ownership: Salary/Owners Draw

What financial gain are you expecting from this business? Not only how much money do you want to make, but how much money can you survive on, and for how long?

To answer these questions your plan's financial projections must be realistic. That's why all elements of your business plan should be thought through…so that you can make a realistic decision on your investment. Everything is connected and has an implication on the bottom line, which as you know, is the amount of money left for you, the owner, to use as your income.

Does your plan allow you to take a salary? First of all, if you are the only employee of your startup as the "Sole Proprietor" or you are part of an owner "Partnership" without other employees, then you wouldn't be taking a salary at all. Instead, all of the company's profit falls into your personal income; that income is not considered a company cost. Your business plan's financial projections, year over year, will determine how much is left for you. Once you develop that, you can then answer if that is enough for you to live on. The amount you take out for your personal spending is called the "owner's draw". You are essentially drawing cash out of the business at any time you want, and paying taxes on it as your personal income during tax time (or throughout the year in monthly or quarterly tax payments).

If you have multiple employees, then *you* can take a salary as well. That salary can be whatever you want it to be. It's important to remember however, that the success of your business over time is not based on how much money you *want* to take from it as a salary, but how much you can *realistically* take as a salary after being able to support the business's operating costs and the realistic compensation of your qualified and capable employees. Your salary as the owner should be the variable one. That means during some years you may not make enough money to take a salary at all. But if successful, you can take as much salary as the business affords. Keep in mind that it should be a reasonable amount compared to comparable companies. You should discuss this with your accountant…but congratulations to you once you are able to have that discussion!

As the owner, you need to have financial flexibility during your startup. A sound business plan will give you the roadmap to determine if you can support yourself and your family during that time when the business is getting off the ground.

Make sure your business plan includes as many years as needed to reach your payment expectation for ownership. If your business plan hits your goal in two years, then a two-three year plan is all you need. If it takes four years, make the plan a 4-5 year plan. Just be realistic about it so you can decide if you can *afford* the results.

There is no "right" answer to this question. Some sole proprietorships make very little profit, however their operating costs offset many expenses for the business owner. In this case, from a tax perspective, your goals may be achieved without much income. In order to understand what benefits apply to your business, we recommend talking with a qualified business accountant to review your plan and define the costs you can and should track to achieve these benefits.

How Will Your Operating Costs & Organizational Structure Change Over the Next 24 Months?

Over the course of your business plan are there any significant changes in costs that occur to support your growth? It's important to explain those changes so that any variation in the financials is clear.

5

BUSINESS RAMP-UP

This section of your business plan defines the starting point of your business and its progression over the course of the business plan. It also provides an opportunity to outline future growth strategies (phases two or three) that would take place beyond the initial business plan, once that plan is successful.

Here is what you need to define:

Geographical Range at Startup

Where is the customer base you are targeting at startup? Is it local, and if so, what is the radius around your operation that you will be reaching out to? Is it regional, national, international? Describe your business geography on day one and how it evolves throughout your business plan.

Startup Targets & Timing

What do you need to do to get your business (business plan) in motion? Itemize this list of activities with target start and completion dates.

Following is an example for a *Wooden Craft* startup:

Action	Start Date	Completion Date
Secure business name& LLC entity	March 1	March 31
Set up social media accounts/pages	March 20	April 30
Secure funds for initial project inventory	March 1	April 30
Place/receive order for material & supplies	May 1	May 15
Set up bank account & online ordering	May 1	May 31
Build product samples	May 16	May 31
Post photos & begin sales campaign	June 1	

Products/Services at Startup

What are the specific products and/or services you will be offering at startup? Describe them each in detail.

Product/Service Targets & Timing

Here is where you take each of the products listed under the "products/services at startup" section and chart out their sales revenue (by product) for each year of the business plan. Below is an example for a *Candle & Soap* company.

	Year 1	Year 2	Year 3
Soy Candles	$28,800	$53,000	$59,000
Bath Salts	$14,400	$24,300	$27,000
Soaps	$ 4,800	$ 7,975	$ 9,000
Total Sales Revenue	**$48,000**	**$82,275**	**$95,000**

This view brings some realism to your yearly sales projections. Many times, whether you are starting your company or have been managing it for 20 years, business leaders have a tendency to forecast increases in a total sales number, rather than looking at what needs to occur in order to add up to that number. By breaking down the product/service sales, you get a better feel for what is practical. Your pricing structure plays a big roll in this view as well. We will get into defining that in the Marketing chapter of this book (Chapter 7).

Investment Requirements for Market Growth

What investments need to be made over the course of the business plan in order to expand the market reach? For example, maybe you started your online business via social marketing (Facebook, Twitter), but by year two of your plan you need to build a website to expand your market reach and achieve an increase in sales revenue from that new market. How much will that cost and when does that investment take place in your plan?

Investment Requirements for Product/Service Growth

What investments need to be made over the course of the business plan in order to expand your list of available products and/or services? For example, if you start a landscaping business and by **year three** plan to expand your business into snowplowing during winter months, that will require an investment in snowplowing equipment, possible licenses, etc.. You would need to detail those items, their costs and timeline into your plan.

Decision Metrics for Expansion Plans

It is important to understand future spending requirements and the sales/profit milestones that need to be met in order to afford them. If you don't meet those milestones, the investments can't be made and the projected revenue from those investments won't be achieved; at least not within the projected timeframe. This section of the business plan is where you define those milestones.

What Scale-Up Are You Planning in 2-3 Years?

This chapter reviewed your starting point, products, descriptions and investments required throughout your plan. Here you should define the natural business scale up that will occur as your business progresses. What is happening as your presence becomes known, and as your products evolve? How & when will this impact your growth?

6

BUSINESS METRICS

This section of your business plan is meant to define the key parameters that will track and measure the plan's success. Business Metrics are essential to keeping you, the business owner, focused on achieving your results. It is so easy to get sidetracked and distracted by opportunities, new ideas, or just the chaos of the day-to-day. But by defining and visually focusing on your key results, you open the door to understanding what's working and what's not, as well as provide yourself with insight to modify your activities if your current activities are not working well enough to achieve your plan. This visibility increases the likelihood of business success because you can see in advance if problems are coming down the road…and fix those problems before it's too late.

Whether you are a sole proprietor or have a full staff of employees, Business Metrics are an essential communication and management tool to drive your results to fruition so you can set new targets that drive your business to the next level.

Here is what you need to define:

Top Three Metrics Used to Manage the Business

You've built your financial targets (revenue goals, profit goals, timing), now choose the three variables that monitor those results. It's important to note that variables are not results. Results are past tense. For example, if you have a monthly sales target of $5,000, metrics are the key functions you need to conduct within the month to hit that $5,000 result. So think backwards – in order for that $5,000 to happen, the business needs to....

Consulting Business Example:

My business plan is to charge $100 for consulting services. If I want to achieve $5,000/month, I will need book 50 consulting hours per month. I assume clients will probably average 20 hours per contract so that means I need about three new client contracts per month. Landing three new clients/contracts per month means I have to get out there introducing myself and my services to potential clients. Assuming I can convert 30% of business development prospects into customers, I'll need to conduct 10 business development presentations per month. If all of that goes as planned, I will achieve $5,000 per month in revenue.

Top Three Metrics to Manage this Consulting Business

1) Business Development Presentations/month

2) New Contracts/month

3) Hours Booked/month

All three metrics are related to one another and linked to achieving the monthly revenue goal. The next step is to define the ***target*** for each metric. Please note that you can have more than three metrics, but it's not recommended to expand this list too much. The process of culling your metrics down to a reasonable number enables you to focus on actions that have the most impact on your results.

Targets for Each Metric

Continuing on with the example defined in the previous section "Top Three Metrics Used to Manage the Business", expand on your metrics by defining specific targets for each. For the *Consulting Business* example let's refer back to the "thinking backwards" process. We outlined the following:

Targets for Each Metric Used to Manage the Consulting Business

1) Business Development Presentations/month = **10**
2) New Contracts/month = **3**
3) Hours Booked/month = **50**

These targets define your (or your employee's) actions during the course of each month. If implemented, and your assumptions were correct, you should achieve your goal. These targets are also your source of data to refer back to if your goals aren't being met; so you can make informed decisions about different tactics you should take if needed. For example, if you hit your target of 10 business development presentations per month, but on average you are only able to convert one of them into a contract, then your assumption of a 30% conversion rate was wrong; instead it was only 10%. So you can either increase your business development target to 30/month, or modify your sales pitch to increase the effectiveness of your message.

The point is, as your business evolves, your targets should evolve with it in an effort to achieve your revenue and profit goals.

Person Responsible for Leading & Driving Each Metric

This is where you assign accountability. Take each metric and assign it to an owner. Someone responsible for doing the work and achieving the results. If you are the one and only, that's ok too.

Criteria Customers Will Judge the Business On?

What are the most important factors your customers will be expecting from your business? Is it product quality, speed of delivery, customer support, range of available products? Define ***why*** customers will want to do business with you versus your competition.

How Will Customer Expectations & Feedback Be Tracked?

Based on what you defined as the "Criteria Customers Will Judge the Business On", how will you monitor whether or not those expectations have been met? This is the biggest factor for getting customers to come back and repeat their business with you, as well as recommend your products or services to others. It is the basis for your growth.

What Reporting Structure Will You Use to Track Metrics/Feedback?

How will you physically track each of your metrics, as well as customer feedback? Will you use an excel file, business development database, business specific software, paper notebook? Whatever your method, decide what it will be and stick with it. You can track your metrics daily, weekly, bi-weekly, etc. It really depends on your business and what works best for you. Just make sure it's not an afterthought!

7

MARKETING PLAN

This section of your business plan defines the group of people that you believe *are* (or *will be*) interested in purchasing your products or services. It details the actions you will take to proactively communicate with those people, and the key messages you will use to convince them to do business with you instead of your competition. The important thing to understand about marketing is that there is no absolute right answer; your marketing plan is not a document set in stone, it's a reference document that supports the marketing process.

The marketing process is based on a combination of collecting consumer data, making educated assumptions from that data, then vetting and adjusting those assumptions over time. Many small business owners get stuck here, or skip over parts of this process because it's out of their comfort zone. Remember, it doesn't have to be perfect, it just needs to be logical.

Here is what you need to define:

Market Definition

Describe the largest group of people that would be interested in purchasing your products or services. This is your largest "target" market, or "market segment".

- Who are they?
- Where are they located?
- Why would they want your product or service?
- How will they make their purchase decision?
- What problem will your product or service solve for them?
- Which product or service of yours will be the most important to them?

Once you have defined your largest "target" market, what are some other "fringe or secondary" markets that may be interested in doing business with you? Answer the same questions for each additional group as you did for your largest target market. These fringe groups are typically smaller than your target market, they might be long shots requiring additional convincing to purchase, or they might be interested in fewer, more targeted products/services than your main target market.

Next, go ahead and give each of your market segments their own distinct name & and rank them in order of importance to your business.

Defining your market segments in detail, ***naming*** each with a unique identifier, and ***categorizing*** them in order of importance is a very important exercise. It sets the stage for your business to participate in and focus on. It also provides a knowledge base to expand upon as your business progresses over time.

Your Markets are comprised of living, ever-changing, dynamic ***people*** that you need to take care of, communicate with and understand. The better your ability to define markets & stay up to speed with them, the more useful your products & services will be, and the more successful your business will become.

Size of the Market for Your Products and Services Today

In the previous section titled "Market Definition", you built out all of your market groups. Here is where you list each market group and ***estimate*** how many potential buyers currently exist in it. Not just the amount of people that you believe will purchase **your** product, but the total number of individuals that exist in each market segment overall. Another way of looking at it is the amount of potential buyers you and your competitors will be competing for.

To calculate your estimates you will have to do some research. Take a look at local, regional or national statistics, industry reports, as well as competitor sales data if publically available. Remember, this is an estimate based upon available information. It's impossible to calculate perfectly accurate numbers, but the more effort you make to justify the figure, the better you will be able to focus your business activities. Just be clear on your logic. Fore example, if you have a landscaping business, your target market may be the number of homeowners within a specific town or within a certain radius of your business. If you offer consulting services for small businesses, your target market will be the number of businesses that exist in the region you are serving. If you are selling a product nationwide you can use demographic data, as well as industry specific reports from associations in your industry.

There is a lot of data available on the Internet, through the Better Business Bureau or local business associations such as the Chamber of Commerce.

Size of the Market for Your Products and Services in Two Years

Here is where you take the market size information from the previous section and estimate if it is growing, decreasing or staying the same, essentially, what is the market size for each market segment YR1, YR2 & YR3. The estimate may be different for each market segment and it's important to understand that trend. If you project a market segment to be decreasing or growing, state the reasons you believe are impacting that change.

Projected Market Share Each Year for Three Years

You have defined your markets and their size over a three-year period. Next step is to show the progression of your business within each market group. This chart is directly linked to the sales forecast in your business plan. Here is an example for a *landscaping business*:

Market Segment: Homeowners Within "Yorkville" City Limits

Market Size: YR1=10,000 YR2=10,500 YR3=11,000

My Market Share (number of customer per year/market size):

YR1= 0.8 % (75/10,000)

YR2= 1.2% (125/10,500)

YR3= 1.9% (200/11,000)

Make sure these figures are aligned with your sales projections. For example, if landscaping jobs average $2,000/job. Then my sales projections should come in around YR1= $150,000; YR2 = $250,000; YR3 = $400,000

Main Competitors & Their Market Share

List your top two to three competitors. If there are more, bucket them into an "other" category. For each competitor provide a description of their business and their focus. Do your best to estimate their market share as well. Use your best guess when information is not available.

Key Strengths and Weaknesses of Competitors

For each competitor you have listed, what are they known to be great for and where are they weak? This information will ultimately be used to learn lessons for your own business, as well as find an opening to make your position unique. You will be defining your unique positions in the next section.

Differentiating Factors Versus the Competition

How is your business different or better than each competitor? This is the basis for your customer/sales messaging. What are the benefits of doing business with you instead of other options available to potential customers?

Future Trends Happening in the Market

Over the course of your business plan, and beyond, what significant changes do you foresee happening? How will those trends impact your products or services, as well as the way you do business?

Pricing Structure

List each product or service that you will be offering, along with its price. Will you offer any discounts, or offer any deals as part of your pricing strategy? What about shipping? Will the customer pay the full shipping cost or is it already included in the purchase price? Here is an example of the pricing structure for a *Candle & Soap* company.

- Soy Candles: $18 per unit
- Bath Salts: $10 per unit
- Soaps: $4 per unit
- Buy two, get one free promotions will take place throughout the year.
- Customer is responsible for all shipping costs.

Product Cost, Also Known as Cost of Goods Sold (COGS)

How much will each of your products cost to produce? If you are a service provider, how much does each service cost to execute? When preparing your product cost you will need to detail the raw materials utilized, both in volume and cost, as well as any labor costs associated with the product's production. If you offer a service you should estimate the average time (in hours) that it takes to perform a service multiplied by the hourly labor cost in order to estimate your total service cost. This will create your COGS per unit or service that will be used to determine your profit margin ((Sales Price – COGS) / Sales Price)). You will also use this information to determine the raw material volumes you need to purchase in order to support your sales plan.

Continuing the example for a *Candle & Soap* company:

Soy Candle		**Bath Salt**		**Soap**	
Soy	$3.00	Salt	$2.00	Melt	$1.00
Container	$1.50	Container	$1.50	Scent	$0.50
Scent	$1.00	Scent	$1.00	Coloring	$0.50
Wick	$0.50	Coloring	$0.75	Packaging	$0.75
COGS	**$6.00**	**COGS**	**$5.25**	**COGS**	**$2.75**
GM	67%	GM	48%	GM	31%

You will notice that labor costs are not included in this COGS calculation. That's because this Sole Proprietorship has no employees. If an employee was hired just to produce products, that salary would be spread out over the product cost.

Distribution Channels

How are your customers going to both purchase and receive their products or services? Are purchases made through a company website, in a local store, through third party distributors? Are products delivered through truck service, the post, local pickup, in store at time of purchase? Are services ordered online, through local meetings, etc.?

Social Media Strategy

Which social media platforms will your business use? How will you manage them? What purpose will each serve? What type of consistent messaging will you project from each platform? Social media can include Facebook, Twitter, LinkedIn and many others. There are so many options that you just can't do everything; decide which make the most sense for your business and have a plan to generate business from them.

Promotional Strategy

Will you place ads in local newspapers, participate in trade associations, use door-to-door flyers, television, direct mail or pay-per-click advertising? What will you do to promote your business and let your target markets know you exist? What will your message be?

Market Accessibility

How easy do you foresee it being to enter into the markets you've defined in your plan? What roadblocks do you need to overcome and what plans do you have to do so?

Business Development

What is your business development strategy and action plan to achieve the actual sales detailed in your business plan? Specifically, what will you do to attract, engage, follow up with and close enough customers to achieve your goals?

8

STARTUP RESOURCES

This section of your business plan details how you will pay for your business and support yourself until your business can make enough money to do both on its own.

Here is what you need to define:

Monthly Income Requirement to Support Current Lifestyle

Obviously it would be great to quadruple your income from your new business, but what's important is to be able to, at a minimum, support your current expenses. Based on your current lifestyle, how much money do you need each month in order to support yourself?

Other Sources of Income During Startup

There is certainly a chance that your business may not make money right away. That being the case, what other sources of income do you have to cover your monthly income requirement?

Savings to Support Yourself During Ramp Up

Do you have money saved that you can draw from to cover your income requirement during startup? If so, how many months will these funds last of no money is coming in?

Other Investors/Partners in the Future

Do you have any partners or investors going into the business with you? What is your plan? Will ownership be shared? How will funds be used? Will you need to repay any of these invested funds?

Loans to Support the Startup Period

Have you, or will you, apply for any loans or grants to fund your business during startup? What are the terms of the loans or grants? How will you pay these funds back?

Owner Investment in the Business

How much of your own personal funds are you investing into the business? In other words, how much money are you willing to lose forever? It sounds harsh and certainly is not your goal, however you need to be prepared for it. When you spend your own money on a small business, there are no guarantees. Is the risk worth it?

Financial Objective

Is the purpose of your business to fully support yourself and your family, or is it a profitable hobby? What is your ultimate financial objective from this business?

Backup Plan

IF your business plan does not come to fruition within the amount of time and money you have allotted, what will you do next? And more importantly, at what point will you need to make the decision to change course?

9

ADMINISTRATIVE RESOURCES

This section of your business plan defines outside services required to support the business, as well as the monthly or yearly fees associated with those services.

Here is what you need to define:

Registered Business Name & Tax ID

Have you set up your company's legal entity? If not, what is your plan? What costs are associated with setup, as well as yearly maintenance? Where are you, or do you plan to be, registered to conduct business?

Registered Patents/Trademarks/Permits

Do you require any patents, trademarks or permits to conduct your business? What is you plan? What is the status/timing of each, as well as the costs & terms of each?

Loans

Do you have, or do you plan to take out, any loans to support the business? Some examples include vehicle loans & construction loans. What are the terms of those loans, as well as principle and interest payments?

Legal Fees

Do you have a business lawyer? What legal costs will your business incur on an annual basis? Does your business require any ongoing operational legal expenses?

Accounting Fees

Do you have an accounting service or tax accountant? What accounting costs will your business incur on an annual basis? Does your business require any ongoing operational accounting expenses?

Healthcare Costs

Does your business need to cover the costs of health insurance for yourself or any employees? What are those monthly fees?

Insurance Costs (other than healthcare)

Do you have or require business insurance? What insurance costs will your business incur on an annual basis? Does your business require any ongoing insurance expenses?

Rent & Utility Costs

Are you renting space for your business to operate in or is it a home-based business? If renting, what is your monthly rent? What are your monthly utility costs such as Internet, phone, security, electricity etc.? If it's a home based business, what utility costs are incurred in addition to the standard utilities used in your home?

Marketing & Promotional Costs

What is your monthly and annual budget linked to your marketing plan? Break this budget out by month & activity, such as social media, print advertising, fliers, website, television, etc. If any expenditure is contingent on achieving sales goals, detail what those goals are. If the expenditures are part of your startup plan, state that as the case.

Other Requirements

Are there any other required services that have significant costs for your business such as association fees, fuel, equipment rental, cleaning services?

10

EMPLOYMENT PLAN

This section of your business plan defines the employees necessary to achieve your goals. If you are forming a company that will not have any employees, then you can skip this section.

Here is what you need to define:

Number of Employees

How many employees will be working for your company at the time of startup and each year throughout the business plan period?

Job Titles & Descriptions

For each job title, describe the job's objectives, responsibilities and desired qualification requirements for potential employees. Qualification requirements can include education and experience required for each job.

Wages

For each job title, provide the annual wage estimate. This can be a fixed number or a wage range. Explain how wages will evolve over the course of the plan. Don't forget to consider payroll taxes in these figures.

Benefits

What, if any, benefits will you offer to employees? Healthcare, insurance, auto allowance, etc.?

Other Requirements

Will employees need to sign a non-compete agreement or take a drug test? Are there any other requirements necessary for potential employees to fulfill before accepting employment with your company?

11

FUTURE EXPANSION PLANS

This section of your business plan defines how your business structure may change over time. Examples of expansion include moving to a larger location, entering into additional geographic regions, as well as adding additional products/services to your mix. Expansions typically happen once growth milestones are reached. This is the longer term, strategic plan for your business; your vision beyond the startup period.

Here is what you need to define:

Plans for Expanding the Current Business Model

What expansion plans do you foresee for your business? What is the timeline for those plans? What business milestones need to be met in order to implement those plans?

Investment Required to Achieve Future Expansion

Based on your future plans (defined in the section above), how much do you estimate the expansion to cost? How will you pay for it?

Business Milestones Required Before Expansion

What specific milestones (business results) must be achieved before you can begin to implement your expansion plans?

Expansion Within the Current Business Plan

Are any of your expansion plans happening within this current business plan? Are the investments identified in your financials?

Business Sustainability

Will your business continue to be sustainable (function profitably and competitively) if no expansion takes place at all?

12

"GUT" CHECK

This section of your business plan defines potential startup risks, how to avoid those risks, as well as a short-term action plan to ensure you succeed in doing so.

Here is what you need to define:

Have You Ever Conducted a Market Test for Your Business?

A market test is just that, discussing or showing your product/service to the group of people you plan on selling to once your business goes "live". It is highly recommended to do this if you haven't done so already. Once completed, describe what was tested and what feedback you received.

If you haven't conducted your market test yet, try giving your product away for free in return for an honest opinion, not only on the product itself, but the price, the ability to order, delivery times, etc. If it's a service you are providing, you can offer your service for free and request similar feedback on the service quality, delivery, communication, price, etc.

Feedback is so important because it gives you an opportunity to tweak your message, product presentation and quality before you open your doors. Without this market test you run the risk of your *new* business receiving negative feedback and a bad reputation. Avoid this risk by getting targeted customer feedback first.

Has Anyone Tried Your Business Idea & Failed?

What is the history of your type of business in terms of failure? Do you know why similar businesses have failed? What lessons can you learn from them so you don't make the same mistakes? It's just as important to understand what has made similar business in your area successful. What lessons can you learn from them so you can achieve similar success with a shorter learning curve?

How is Your Business Plan Different and/or Better Than Similar Businesses?

What makes your business unique? Did you test this uniqueness during your market test? How did customers react? Do customers believe there is value in that differentiating factor? What was that value as defined by the customer?

It's important to define these positive differences so that they are part of your communication, marketing and customer connections. When you don't define valuable differences, or define them incorrectly, you run the risk of losing the best opportunity you have to make your business known and remembered. Ultimately slowing down or hindering your success.

When You Launch Your Business: What Will You Do In Your First Month?

A strong start to your business is crucial because it's the basis for your momentum going forward. Considering all of the elements of your business plan, focusing on the sales & financial forecast for the ***first three months***, what specific actions will you take to achieve those results?

When You Launch Your Business: What Will You Do Months Two Through Six?

Considering all of the elements of your business plan, focusing on the sales & financial forecast for ***months three-six***, what specific actions will you take to achieve those results?

When You Launch Your Business: What Will You Do Months Six Through Twelve?

Considering all of the elements of your business plan, focusing on the sales & financial forecast for ***month's six-twelve***, what specific actions will you take to achieve those results?

Businesses are not successful just because their products or services are available, it takes a lot of work. When you plan specific actions aligned with achieving specific results, you have an opportunity to Gut Check whether or not your plan is realistic. Without this process, you run the risk of planning unrealistic sales and profit expectations and exhausting your funds before your business even gets off the ground.

Where Do You Need Help?

Once your business plan is complete and your monthly action plan is established, think about where you are *least comfortable* with what needs to be done. What are your own personal weaknesses? To assume you know everything there is to know about running a business on your own is simply naive. Everyone needs help, support, or just someone to bounce ideas off of. What is your support network? What are your weak points and how are you going to strengthen each one of them?

By thinking this through and identifying resources in advance, you avoid the risk of falling short in those areas and getting stuck there. Making a business successful means using time wisely so you can earn a profit on schedule. Set yourself up for success by building a resource network now. This can include individuals, trade groups, taking a class, reading a book, etc.

What is Your Biggest Fear or Question Moving Forward?

Hopefully you are confident in your plan, have thought through the risks already and have contingencies in place to overcome them. If, however, at this point you still have fears or questions, write them down and take the time to address them; making changes to your plan if necessary.

Starting a business is a big deal, it's fulfilling a dream, and that's not something to enter into lightly. Make sure this section is empty before you get started.

13

INVESTMENT BREAKDOWN

This section of your business plan defines the specific items you need to purchase in order to start your business. It's important to itemize costs and timelines for each purchase, as well as consider more than one investment path so that you have options just incase adjustments need to be made.

Here is what you need to define:

What Assets Do You Need to Purchase to Get Your Business Started?

An asset can be a piece of equipment, computer, furniture, vehicle, a building, raw material inventory, finished goods inventory, etc. If your business is web based, the website itself is considered an asset. These are tangible items that you need to own in order to get your business running. First describe each asset in detail and estimate a cost. Next, take the time to consider *cost options*. What is the cost of the asset if purchased new versus used? Does the asset need to be purchased prior to the start of the business, within the first three months, or three years? Is there a specific business milestone that needs to be achieved before this asset actually gets utilized? If so, you can plan the timing for that purchase once the financial milestone is achieved instead of buying it now and having it sit idle until a future date.

The point is, the less startup capital you put into the business, the better. It is very easy to spend too much, too soon. Plan it out and be realistic, keeping in mind the "goal" is to spend your startup capital on necessary items only. Once you have culled this down to mandatory items, what is the total investment required and do you have the money available to purchase these items?

What Operating Expenses Will You Need to Pay Out-of-Pocket Until the Business Can Support Them on Its Own?

Operating Expenses are monthly costs required for the business to function. These can include rent, phone or Internet service, fuel, marketing/advertising costs, utilities, labor, insurance, loan payments, etc. You will need to itemize each cost on a monthly basis and determine how many months you will need to fund these activities with your own money until the business can generate enough income to pay for them on its own. What does that add up to and do you have that money available to use?

What Other Startup Expenses Will You Need to Fund?

Other expenses can include legal fees, licenses, etc. What is the total cost and do you have the money available to support these expenses?

Chart Your Investment Plan

In this "Investment Breakdown" section of your business plan, you've defined the assets, operating costs & other startup expenses that require funding from sources outside of the business. That can include your life savings, a bank loan, funds from outside investors or small business grants. Whatever the funding source, there is one common element…these funds are not generated by the business itself and there is no guarantee of getting paid back. This is the risk of starting a business, and the reason why aligning your budget and action plan is so essential to reducing that risk.

Most business plans show a financial breakdown of two, three or four years from the start of business. It's important, however, to chart your Investment Plan, prior to that time frame so that you, the business owner, fully understand what funds you need to put into this to make it work.

Here's an example of an Investment Plan for an *Ice Cream Parlor*, ***$152,800*** in Year Zero (in this case 6 months prior to launch).

	- 6 Months	**- 5 Months**	**- 4 Months**	**- 3 Months**	**- 2 Months**	**- 1 Months**
Assets						
Building	$90,000	$20,000	$10,000	$ 5,000		
Furnishings					$10,000	
Systems					$ 2,500	
Inventory						$ 700
Subtotal	*$90,000*	*$20,000*	*$10,000*	*$ 5,000*	*$12,500*	*$ 700*
Operating Costs						
Utilities		$ 500	$ 500	$ 500	$ 500	$ 500
Labor					$ 2,000	$ 2,000
Marketing					$ 900	$ 1,500
Subtotal		*$ 500*	*$ 500*	*$ 500*	*$ 3,400*	*$ 4,000*
Other						
Closing Costs	$ 4,000					
Legal					$ 1,200	
Licenses					$ 500	
Subtotal	*$ 4,000*				*$ 1,700*	
Grand Total	**$94,000**	**$20,500**	**$10,500**	**$ 5,500**	**$17,600**	**$ 4,700**

In the *Ice Cream Parlor* example, startup costs total $152,800. There is a six-month timeline, prior to the business launch, when the money will need to be spent. This business owner needs to make some decisions. How much will be covered by personal savings, taking a loan, etc.? Is the total amount feasible and how exactly will it be funded?

As you answer these questions for your own business, you can go back and modify your plan until you are fully comfortable with the result. You can start by reviewing the investment options that you detailed out in this section. Maybe you purchase second hand furnishings instead of new. Maybe you lease space instead of purchase a building. Thinking this through in advance will set you, and your business up for success. Who knows, maybe you'll find that you don't need used equipment and can afford that new item right away!

In the next chapter we will review your month-by-month financials. This is the revenue, expenses and profitability chart for the course of your planning period (two, three or four years). Once you've detailed that plan, make sure you come back here and extend your *investment breakdown* IF your revenue is not enough to cover your operating expenses over the first few months. You may need more of your own cash to fund these expenses until the business generates enough to do so on its own.

14

FINANCIALS

This section of your business plan defines the income and cash flow projection for your business startup. It will tell the story of your business in the form of a spreadsheet, showing the sales evolution of specific products or services, the operating expenses in relationship to sales, and most importantly, ***when*** and ***how much*** profit your business will make.

One of the first questions anyone asks before starting this process is "how many years should be projected in the plan?" Well, that depends on how much money you put in. Your business plan needs to project as many years as it takes for your business's profit to pay off the initial financial investment. For example, if you put $30,000 of your savings into a small business start up and that startup generates an average of $1,500 in profit per month, it will take 20 months to pay off that investment ($30,000 / $1,500 = 20 months). In this case a two year business plan (24 months) would be adequate because the business shows that it is self-sufficient within that period. That being said, three years is still preferable to show how the business will evolve; not necessary, but recommended.

Using that same $30,000 investment example, let's say the average monthly profit is $500. In this case it would take 60 months to pay off that investment ($30,000 / $500 = 60 months). That would require a minimum of five years to start generating profit beyond your initial investment. The plan should then be at least five years.

If you take out a loan for your business startup and incorporate those loan payments into your business expenses, then that portion of your payback period will be whatever the terms of your loan are, and the business plan period should accommodate those terms. What we often forget however, is paying ourselves back for the personal funds we put into the startup. Make sure your plan goes out as long as it takes to pay yourself back. Why is that important? Simply put…you need to be honest with yourself, and about the value of your money.

Let's say you quit your job to start your own business and in the process invest $105,000 of your retirement savings in order to make that dream a reality. If your business plan calculates seven years to pay back that initial investment before you are able to start making any ***new*** money (roughly $15,000 per year after 7 years), can you afford that? Essentially using $105,000 of money you already have, to make an additional $15,000 of new money almost eight years later? If your business a hobby that you love and you are willing to spend $105,000 to do something you love to do, then great, it makes sense. But if your intention is to support yourself and your family, you may decide to invest your money elsewhere or go down a different path.

Small business owners are often asked, "is this a hobby or a business?" In the case of the above example, you would have to say hobby because of the low profit and extended time frame. A successful business should have a payback of no more than three years, one to two years being ideal. And it should generate enough ***new profit***, per month & year, to achieve the business owner's financial goal, whatever you define that goal to be.

The value of money is not the only negative factor of an extended payback period. The other risk factor is change in the market. The market your business participates in is bound to evolve over time with new competition, different product or service alternatives, new trends, etc. Money should always be paid back within a reasonable timeframe so that the likelihood of changed market factors is limited.

Bottom line when it comes to building your business plan's financial statement is the following:

- Have a financial goal for your business.
- Use specific details from your business plan story (chapters 1-13) to populate your financial plan.
- Extend your plan as long as it takes to pay back your initial investment.
- Determine if your result reaches your financial goals. If not, make adjustments to the plan itself (not just the financials).

This last point is really important. It's too easy to increase your monthly sales figures so that your goals are met in the financial spreadsheet. But does your plan realistically support achieving those numbers? Maybe finding a way to reduce costs is a better first step in getting to your profit goals. Just make sure those changes are updated and supported throughout your plan.

Here is what you need to define:

Customize Your Financial Spreadsheet

Your business plan's financial spreadsheet is not a document that is used during the planning process and then ignored once your business is functioning. Instead, the format you build here is the format you will use to manage your business going forward. Your plan is what you are aiming to achieve. The format then becomes a blank template to input your actual monthly results. You will be able to compare results to your original plan and adjust your activities to ensure goals are met.

The next page shows an example of a customized financial spreadsheet for a *Candle & Soap* company.

Let's start with a ***Sales Plan***. The sales plan consists of sales volume (units sold) & revenue projections for year one of the business plan based on the business plan's price structure.

Price Structure (as defined in the Marketing Plan, Chapter 7):

- Soy Candles: $18 per unit
- Bath Salts: $10 per unit
- Soaps: $4 per unit
- Buy two, get one free promotions will take place throughout the year.

Sales Volume Projection (# of Units Sold)

Volume	Jan	Feb	Mar	Apr	May	Jun	Jul	Aug	Sept	Oct	Nov	Dec	Total
Soy Candles	28	39	50	67	89	111	128	161	183	222	244	278	1,600
Bath Salts	10	20	40	60	90	120	140	160	180	190	210	220	1,440
Soaps	19	31	50	63	81	100	106	119	125	138	163	206	1,200
Total Units Sold	**57**	**90**	**140**	**189**	**260**	**331**	**374**	**440**	**488**	**550**	**617**	**704**	**4,240**

Sales Revenue Projection (# of Units Sold x Price Per Unit)

Revenue	Jan	Feb	Mar	Apr	May	Jun	Jul	Aug	Sept	Oct	Nov	Dec	Total
Soy Candles	$500	$700	$900	$1.200	$1,600	$2,000	$2,300	$2,900	$3,300	$4,000	$4,400	$5,000	$28,800
Bath Salts	$100	$200	$400	$600	$900	$1,200	$1,400	$1,600	$1,800	$1,900	$2,100	$2,200	$14,400
Soaps	$75	$125	$200	$250	$325	$400	$425	$475	$500	$550	$650	$825	$4,800
Discounts	$203	$308	$450	$0	$0	$0	$0	$0	$0	$0	$0	$2,408	$3,368
Total Revenue	$473	$718	$1,050	$2,050	$2,825	$3,600	$4,125	$4,975	$5,600	$6,450	$7,150	$5,618	$44,633

Next let's add ***Cost of Goods Sold (COGS)***. The cost plan consists of raw material costs incurred to produce the volume of product sold by product type. First you need to detail your costs per product type, then multiply that cost per product volume.

Product Cost (as defined in the Marketing Plan, Chapter 7):

- Soy Candles: $6.00 per unit
- Bath Salts: $5.25 per unit
- Soaps: $2.75 per unit
- Customer is responsible for all shipping costs.

COGS Projection (# of Units Sold x Cost Per Unit)

COGS	Jan	Feb	Mar	Apr	May	Jun	Jul	Aug	Sept	Oct	Nov	Dec	Total
Soy Candles	$167	$233	$300	$400	$533	$667	$767	$967	$1,100	$1,333	$1,467	$1,667	$9,600
Bath Salts	$53	$105	$210	$315	$473	$630	$735	$840	$945	$998	$1,103	$1,155	$7,560
Soaps	$52	$86	$138	$172	$233	$275	$292	$327	$344	$378	$447	$567	$3,300
Total COGS	**$271**	**$424**	**$648**	**$887**	**$1,229**	**$1,572**	**$1,794**	**$2,133**	**$2,389**	**$2,709**	**$3,016**	**$3,389**	**$20,460**

Gross Income Projection (Sales Revenue - COGS)

Gross Margin % Projection (GM $ / Sales Revenue)

Gross Margin	Jan	Feb	Mar	Apr	May	Jun	Jul	Aug	Sept	Oct	Nov	Dec	Total
Gross Income	$202	$293	$403	$1,163	$1,596	$2,028	$2,331	$2,842	$3,211	$3,741	$4,134	$2,229	$24,173
GM %	43%	41%	38%	57%	56%	56%	57%	57%	57%	58%	58%	40%	54%

After calculating your Gross Margin it's time to take a look at ***Payroll Costs.*** Payroll consists of any part or full time employees working for the company. The *Candle & Soap* company does not have any employees so this section would be left blank. The owner is not taking a salary, instead they will take an owner's draw from company profits. That will not show up in this section. So for the sake of this example, let's take a look at the *Consulting Firm* we reviewed in chapter four. This firm has five full time employees and several consulting contractors. The contractors are paid for their time spent on specific jobs, not a salary. So contractor rates are calculated into the COGS model, and not payroll. The full time staff however is considered payroll. First we break down the team, then break monthly payroll out for the financial plan.

Employee List (as defined in the Organizational Structure, Chapter 4):

Name	Title	Monthly Salary	Yearly Salary	Status
John Smith	Owner	$8,333	$100,000	full time
Laura Smith	Owner	$8,333	$100,000	full time
Sarah Block	Team Mgr.	$6,667	$80,000	full time
Jeb Larson	Trainer	$5,417	$65,000	full time
Sam Parker	Cust. Serv.	$4,167	$50,000	full time
		$32,917	**$395,000**	

Payroll (Wages and Payroll Taxes)

Payroll	Jan	Feb	Mar	Apr	May	Jun	Jul	Aug	Sept	Oct	Nov	Dec	Total
Payroll	$32,917	$32,917	$32,917	$32,917	$32,917	$32,917	$32,917	$32,917	$32,917	$32,917	$32,917	$32,917	**$395,000**
Payroll Tax	$3,292	$3,292	$3,292	$3,292	$3,292	$3,292	$3,292	$3,292	$3,292	$3,292	$3,292	$3,292	**$39,500**
Total Payroll	**$36,208**	**$36,208**	**$36,208**	**$36,208**	**$36,208**	**$36,208**	**$36,208**	**$36,208**	**$36,208**	**$36,208**	**$36,208**	**$36,208**	**$434,500**

The next section of the financial breakdown is ***Operating Expenses***. These are the monthly costs associated with keeping the lights on and the business functioning. Operating expenses can include office supplies, rent, telephone, internet, repairs & maintenance, cleaning service, fuel, marketing fees, auto lease, etc. Basically, any cost other than COGS and payroll. Here is an example of Operating Expenses for the *Candle & Soap* company.

Operating Expenses

Operating Expenses	Jan	Feb	Mar	Apr	May	Jun	Jul	Aug	Sept	Oct	Nov	Dec	Total
Telephones	$250	$250	$250	$250	$250	$250	$250	$250	$250	$250	$250	$250	$3,000
Internet	$75	$75	$75	$75	$75	$75	$75	$75	$75	$75	$75	$75	$900
Supplies	$300	$50	$50	$50	$50	$50	$50	$50	$50	$50	$50	$50	$850
Website	$7,000	$3,000	$200	$200	$200	$200	$200	$200	$200	$200	$200	$200	12,000
Marketing Advertising	$300	$300	$300	$300	$300	$300	$300	$300	$300	$300	$300	$300	$3,600
Rent	$0	$0	$0	$0	$0	$0	$0	$0	$0	$0	$0	$0	$0
Insurance	$450	$0	$0	$450	$0	$0	$450	$0	$0	$450	$0	$0	$1,800
Accounting	$0	$0	$700	$0	$0	$0	$0	$0	$0	$0	$0	$0	$700
Legal	$300	$0	$0	$0	$0	$0	$0	$0	$0	$0	$0	$0	$300
Total Operating Expenses	**$8,675**	**$3,675**	**$1,575**	**$1,325**	**$875**	**$875**	**$1,325**	**$875**	**$875**	**$1,325**	**$875**	**$875**	**$23,150**

Net Income Projection (Gross Income – Payroll – Operating Expenses)

Net Margin % Projection (NI $ / Sales Revenue)

Net Margin	Jan	Feb	Mar	Apr	May	Jun	Jul	Aug	Sept	Oct	Nov	Dec	Total
Net Income	-$8,473	-$3,382	-$1,173	-$162	$721	$1,153	$1,006	$1,967	$2,336	$2,416	$3,259	$1,354	$1,023
NM %	-1793%	-471%	-112%	-8%	26%	32%	24%	40%	42%	37%	46%	24%	2%

Taxes

The above example shows the financial result before taxes. In this case, it's a home based business, sole proprietorship, so 'end of year' Net Income (profit) of $1,023 would be added to the owners income, and personal income taxes would be paid on that amount.

Please note that the sales tax must also be accounted for since this is a retail product. In this case the *Candle & Soap* company charges sales tax and shipping costs at the time of purchase to be paid by the customer in addition to the product price. The company is responsible for sending quarterly sales tax payments to the government, however they are not shown in this example as it's a separate transaction.

If your business is required to pay sales tax, make sure you are aware of the rules and rates in your home state and any additional states you will be doing business in. You may be required to obtain permits to collect taxes, as well as receive the appropriate tax forms to file monthly or quarterly returns.

Tying It All Together

On the next page we will take all the financial statement components and create a cohesive Income Statement. Take a look at it and then let's examine the story behind it.

FULL Financial Income Statement <u>YEAR 1</u>: Candle & Soap Company

Revenue	Jan	Feb	Mar	Apr	May	Jun	Jul	Aug	Sept	Oct	Nov	Dec	Total
Soy Candles	$500	$700	$900	$1,200	$1,600	$2,000	$2,300	$2,900	$3,300	$4,000	$4,400	$5,000	$28,800
Bath Salts	$100	$200	$400	$600	$900	$1,200	$1,400	$1,600	$1,800	$1,900	$2,100	$2,200	$14,400
Soaps	$75	$125	$200	$250	$325	$400	$425	$475	$500	$550	$650	$825	$4,800
Discounts	$203	$308	$450	$0	$0	$0	$0	$0	$0	$0	$0	$2,408	$3,368
Total Revenue	$473	$718	$1,050	$2,050	$2,825	$3,600	$4,125	$4,975	$5,600	$6,450	$7,150	$5,618	$44,633
Soy Candles	$167	$233	$300	$400	$533	$667	$767	$967	$1,100	$1,333	$1,467	$1,667	$9,600
Bath Salts	$53	$105	$210	$315	$473	$630	$735	$840	$945	$998	$1,103	$1,155	$7,560
Soaps	$52	$86	$138	$172	$233	$275	$292	$327	$344	$378	$447	$567	$3,300
Total COGS	**$271**	**$424**	**$648**	**$887**	**$1,229**	**$1,572**	**$1,794**	**$2,133**	**$2,389**	**$2,709**	**$3,016**	**$3,389**	**$20,460**
Gross Income	202	293	403	1,163	1,596	2,028	2,331	2,842	3,211	3,741	4,134	2,229	24,173
GM %	43%	41%	38%	57%	56%	56%	57%	57%	57%	58%	58%	40%	54%
Payroll	$0	$0	$0	$0	$0	$0	$0	$0	$0	$0	$0	$0	$0
Payroll Tax	$0	$0	$0	$0	$0	$0	$0	$0	$0	$0	$0	$0	$0
Total Payroll	$0	$0	$0	$0	$0	$0	$0	$0	$0	$0	$0	$0	$0
Telephones	$250	$250	$250	$250	$250	$250	$250	$250	$250	$250	$250	$250	$3,000
Internet	$75	$75	$75	$75	$75	$75	$75	$75	$75	$75	$75	$75	$900
Supplies	$300	$50	$50	$50	$50	$50	$50	$50	$50	$50	$50	$50	$850
Website	$7,000	$3,000	$200	$200	$200	$200	$200	$200	$200	$200	$200	$200	12,000
Marketing Advertising	$300	$300	$300	$300	$300	$300	$300	$300	$300	$300	$300	$300	$3,600
Rent	$0	$0	$0	$0	$0	$0	$0	$0	$0	$0	$0	$0	$0
Insurance	$450	$0	$0	$450	$0	$0	$450	$0	$0	$450	$0	$0	$1,800
Accounting	$0	$0	$700	$0	$0	$0	$0	$0	$0	$0	$0	$0	$700
Legal	$300	$0	$0	$0	$0	$0	$0	$0	$0	$0	$0	$0	$300
Total Operating Expenses	**$8,675**	**$3,675**	**$1,575**	**$1,325**	**$875**	**$875**	**$1,325**	**$875**	**$875**	**$1,325**	**$875**	**$875**	**$23,150**
Net Income	-$8,473	-$3,382	-$1,173	-$162	$721	$1,153	$1,006	$1,967	$2,336	$2,416	$3,259	$1,354	$1,023
NM %	-1793%	-471%	-112%	-8%	26%	32%	24%	40%	42%	37%	46%	24%	2%

What Story Does Your Financial Statement Tell?

Your Business Plan's Financial Statement should tell the story of where you are going and when you are going to get there. It also serves as a template for tracking month-over-month results as you enter actual data and compare monthly results with your original plan. Once you know how to read it properly, you will have a clear view of potential obstacles and opportunities that you can plan & adjust for in advance.

Let's review the story of the *Candle & Soap* company's Year 1 Financial Statement. Below are some key points. See if you can reference them back to the spreadsheet.

- ✓ The company plans to sell three different product types, Candles, Salts and Soaps totaling $44,633 in sales revenue it's first year.
- ✓ Soy Candles are the largest income generator for the business with the largest gross margin.
- ✓ The cost to produce the product is relatively low with a gross margin of close to 60% (when sold at full price).
- ✓ The company plans to offer several price discounts to generate sales during the ramp up and holiday periods.
- ✓ There are no employees at this point and the owner is able to produce all products on his own.
- ✓ The operation is home based without any rent expenses.
- ✓ The upfront costs of setting up the website and establishing supplies will require an initial capital investment of about $15,000 until the business begins to support itself.

- ✓ The business begins to support itself in the fifth month of operation and projects to earn $1,023 by year end.

- ✓ The $15,000 investment will take more than one year to pay off so at least one an additional year of business plan must be accounted for.

FULL Financial Income Statement YEAR 2: Candle & Soap Company

Revenue	Jan	Feb	Mar	Apr	May	Jun	Jul	Aug	Sept	Oct	Nov	Dec	Total
Soy Candles	$4,000	$4,000	$4,000	$5,000	$5,000	$4,000	$4,000	$4,000	$4,000	$5,000	$5,000	$5,000	$53,000
Bath Salts	$1,900	$1,900	$1,900	$2,200	$2,200	$1,900	$1,900	$1,900	$1,900	$2,200	$2,200	$2,200	$24,300
Soaps	$550	$550	$550	$825	$825	$550	$550	$550	$550	$825	$825	$825	$7,975
Discounts	$1,935	$1,935	$1,935	$0	$0	$0	$0	$0	$0	$0	$0	$2,408	$8,213
Total Revenue	$4,515	$4,515	$4,515	$8,025	$8,025	$6,450	$6,450	$6,450	$6,450	$8,025	$8,025	$5,618	$77,063
Soy Candles	$1,333	$1,333	$1,333	$1,667	$1,667	$1,333	$1,333	$1,333	$1,333	$1,667	$1,667	$1,667	**$17,667**
Bath Salts	$998	$998	$998	$1,155	$1,155	$998	$998	$998	$998	$1,155	$1,155	$1,155	**$12,758**
Soaps	$378	$378	$378	$567	$567	$378	$378	$378	$378	$567	$567	$567	**$5,843**
Total COGS	**$2,709**	**$2,709**	**$2,709**	**$3,389**	**$3,389**	**$2,709**	**$2,709**	**$2,709**	**$2,709**	**$3,389**	**$3,389**	**$3,389**	**$35,907**
Gross Income	$1,806	$1,806	$1,806	$4,636	$4,636	$3,741	$3,741	$3,741	$3,741	$4,636	$4,636	$2,229	$41,156
GM %	40%	40%	40%	58%	58%	58%	58%	58%	58%	58%	58%	40%	53%
Payroll	$0	$0	$0	$0	$0	$0	$0	$0	$0	$0	$0	$0	$0
Payroll Tax	$0	$0	$0	$0	$0	$0	$0	$0	$0	$0	$0	$0	$0
Total Payroll	$0	$0	$0	$0	$0	$0	$0	$0	$0	$0	$0	$0	$0
Telephones	$250	$250	$250	$250	$250	$250	$250	$250	$250	$250	$250	$250	$3,000
Internet	$75	$75	$75	$75	$75	$75	$75	$75	$75	$75	$75	$75	$900
Supplies	$300	$50	$50	$50	$50	$50	$50	$50	$50	$50	$50	$50	$850
Website	$200	$200	$200	$200	$200	$200	$200	$200	$200	$200	$200	$200	$2,400
Marketing Advertising	$300	$300	$300	$300	$300	$300	$300	$300	$300	$300	$300	$300	$3,600
Rent	$0	$0	$0	$0	$0	$0	$0	$0	$0	$0	$0	$0	$0
Insurance	$450	$0	$0	$450	$0	$0	$450	$0	$0	$450	$0	$0	$1,800
Accounting	$0	$0	$700	$0	$0	$0	$0	$0	$0	$0	$0	$0	$700
Legal	$300	$0	$0	$0	$0	$0	$0	$0	$0	$0	$0	$0	$300
Total Operating Expenses	**$1,875**	**$875**	**$1,575**	**$1,325**	**$875**	**$875**	**$1,325**	**$875**	**$875**	**$1,325**	**$875**	**$875**	**$13,550**
Net Income	-$69	$931	$231	$3,311	$3,761	$2,866	$2,416	$2,866	$2,866	$3,311	$3,761	$1,354	$27,606
NM %	-2%	21%	5%	41%	47%	44%	37%	44%	44%	41%	47%	24%	36%

What Story Does Your Financial Statement Tell During YEAR 2?

We determined from the Year 1 financial statement for the *Candle & Soap* company that a second year financial statement was necessary in order to ensure the business was making "new money" beyond the initial $15,000 investment.

Let's review the story of the *Candle & Soap* company's Year 2 Financial Statement. Below are some key points. See if you can reference them back to the spreadsheet.

- ✓ The company will continue to sell its original product range with three different product types, Candles, Salts and Soaps totaling $77,063 in sales revenue it's second year. That is a 73% increase in sales.
- ✓ Sales are consistent with the last quarter of Year 1, with some seasonal upswings in the spring and fall holiday seasons.
- ✓ Sales discounts continue to be offered during seasonal promotions.
- ✓ Operating expenses have decreased since the website is now in maintenance mode. This has had a significant effect on Net Margin.
- ✓ Net Margin has increased from 2% at the end of the first year to 36% in year two due to stabilized operating costs.
- ✓ The owner's initial investment of $15,000 will be fully paid off by the month of August during the second year of operation. That equates to a very strong 1.8 month rate of return on investment.
- ✓ From September through December of YEAR 2 the business will generate $11,292 of new money.

- ✓ It is safe to say that IF this business plan is carried out successfully, and YEAR 3 is similar to YEAR 2, the business will generate $27,606 in Net Income. A fully self-sufficient business with a net margin of 36%.

15

EXECUTIVE SUMMARY

This section of your business plan provides an overview of the Who, What, Why, How & When of the business. It is the first section you read at the beginning of the plan, however it is the last section you write when preparing the plan itself. The Executive Summary is just that, a summary of the business plan. Everything in the summary should come from the plan itself, don't reinvent the wheel.

Here is what you need to define:

Who & What

Who is the ownership? What is the business? This is a summary of the "General Business Information" section detailed in Chapter One.

Why & How

Why does this business have a future? How will the business make that future a reality? This is a summary of your marketing plan explaining both the market opportunity and how you will access the market.

When

When will the business start? When will the business achieve growth milestones? When will the business make a profit? This is a summary of the financial plan.

Length of the Executive Summary

The executive summary can be as long as two pages, or as short as two paragraphs, it depends on how much detail you have in your plan. Don't try to fit your executive summary into some format, just answer the questions Who, What, Why, How & When in a concise manner.

16

COMMON RISKS & OPPORTUNITIES

Congratulations! You've completed your Business Plan and are now ready to live out your dream. Before you get started, let's take time to review some common risks and opportunities that can hinder *or help* you along the way.

Once you've reviewed them, you can go back to your plan and see if any adjustments need to be made.

Here are some things to consider:

Risks

1) The sales plan is too aggressive during the first few months of operation. One of the biggest risks to any business plan is that sales start out very strong right away. Unless you have taken "pre-orders" for your business before it opens its doors, your first month's sales are not going to be fantastic. It takes time to generate sales. It takes time to get the word out to new potential customers. Make sure your plan supports this launch time.

2) The sales plan looks like hockey stick. A hockey stick plan appears to

support a business launch with flat to zero sales during the first couple of months then jumps up and continues to climb at a rapid pace month over month. This type of sales plan does not take seasonality into account. Any business has months that are stronger than others, or weaker than others depending on market buying patters. Make sure your plan accounts for this as well.

3) No real business development plan exists. "If you build it they will come" is a falsity. Any new business needs to have a clear strategy with actions associated in order to define, find, engage and close customers. Not just random customers, but the amount of customers needed to achieve your sales plan. Make sure business development is defined in your marketing plan.

4) Your operating costs are unrealistic. Have you considered all of the costs detailed throughout the plan? Try going section by section and verifying you have a cost associated with each activity outlined in your business plan. These should be line items in your financial evaluation.

5) Your pricing is not competitive. It's a common misconception that you can price products or services based on how much it costs the business to provide them. Supply and demand does not work that way. It's important to understand what your competitors are charging and make sure your pricing is within that range. Make sure your pricing represents your product's value in relation to competitive pricing.

6) Your business systems don't support the plan. Make sure you take accounting, managing customer information, order processing, etc. into consideration, as well as the costs associated with it. You can't

successfully manage a business in your head, at least not for long. So be sure to put realistic tools in place to help you achieve your goals.

7) Your business does not achieve its intent. Go back and take a look at the "General Information" section of your plan. Specifically, why are you interested in this business? Have you met your goals? Are you satisfied with the projected results in your plan? Make sure the answer is yes, before you invest.

Opportunities

1) Know you niche. Take the time to research competitors and the market, as well as define why your products are different and why that difference is important to customers. Use this information to position your marketing and business development efforts.

2) Test your product or service concepts before finalizing your business plan. Getting feedback is HUGE. Make sure your perspective is valid by getting affirmation from potential clients without any bias. Consider giving products or services away for free in order to get real feedback so you can make improvements and get your message just right before you launch.

3) Be prepared to monitor your results. Chapter Six discusses "Business Metrics". When you establish how you are going to track the success of your actions, you will increase your power to make desired results come to fruition.

4) Keep your spending options open & as much money in your pockets as you can, for as long as you can. It is impossible to know everything that you need to know before you start your business.

That's why it's so important to have backup options in place when it comes to where you spend your money and how much you spend at one time. Spread out your funds. Allow your business to make money and support its own investment. If you do too much too soon, you may regret an expense and not be able to fund its correction. Keeping your options open will allow you the time to make more informed decisions as you go.

5) Plan ahead to take your dream one step further. If, and when, you meet your goals, what's next? It's a good idea to start planning in advance so that when you achieve key milestones, you know what to do and are able to keep that great momentum going.

17

SMALL BUSINESS PLAN TEMPLATE

It's time to get started. As you read through this book, use this section to begin scripting your business plan. You can expand on it later, but it's important to capture your ideas as you go.

And remember…there is no perfect business plan. Your plan is meant to be a framework for your ideas, so that you can think through everything and get a better understanding of those areas that may be new to you, or those areas that you don't have extensive experience in. Your business plan serves as an important step in the process of making decisions about your future.

Use this template for taking notes right here in the book so that you can start building that framework for your business as you go.

Good luck!

GENERAL BUSINESS INFORMATION

Primary Ownership & Status

Experience

Company Name

Why Are You Interested In This Business?

How Did You Come Up With The Idea?

Industry Description

Monthly Revenue "Today"

Products & Services

Target Revenue In 24 Months

Current Business Status

What Will The Largest Revenue Generator Be For Your Business?

What Part of Your Business Is Not Easily Found In Other Businesses?

What Part of Your Business Cannot Be Replaced By A Competitor?

What Part Of Your Business Cannot Be Duplicated Without Significant Investment?

BUSINESS & FINANCIAL OBJECTIVES

Startup/Investment & Other Capital Requirements

Projected Rate Of Return On Investment

Estimated Operating Costs & Payroll

Estimated Breakeven & Profitability Points

BUSINESS SYSTEMS

Order Management & Processing Systems

Accounting System

Purchasing System

Payroll System

Project Management & Production Systems

Product/Service Delivery & Quality Control

Client Acquisition & Maintenance

System Evolution

OPERATING COSTS & ORGANIZATIONAL STRUCTURE

Principles: Management Expertise & Relevance to the Business

In-House Services VS Outsourced

Responsibility Matrix

Access to Labor Over Ramp-Up Period

Office/Operating Space Requirement & Plan

Patents, Insurance, Legal Requirements/Permits & Licenses

Payment Expectations for Ownership: Salary/Owners Draw

How Will Your Operating Costs & Organizational Structure Change Over the Next 24 Months?

BUSINESS RAMP-UP

Geographical Range at Startup

Startup Targets & Timing

Action	Start Date	Completion Date

Products/Services at Startup

Product/Service Targets & Timing

	Year 1	**Year 2**	**Year 3**

Investment Requirements for Market Growth

Investment Requirements for Product/Service Growth

Decision Metrics for Expansion Plans

What Scale-Up Are You Planning in 2-3 Years?

Business Metrics

Top Three Metrics Used to Manage the Business

Targets for Each Metric

Person Responsible for Leading & Driving Each Metric

Criteria Customers Will Judge the Business On?

How Will Customer Expectations & Feedback Be Tracked?

What Reporting Structure Will You Use to Track Metrics/Feedback?

MARKETING PLAN

Market Definition

Size of the Market for Your Products and Services Today

Size of the Market for Your Products and Services ***in Two Years***

Projected Market Share Each Year for Three Years

Main Competitors & Their Market Share

Key Strengths and Weaknesses of Competitors

Differentiating Factors Versus the Competition

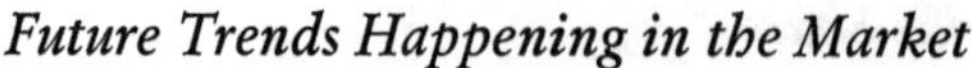

Future Trends Happening in the Market

Pricing Structure

Product Cost, Also Known as Cost of Goods Sold (COGS)

Distribution Channels

Social Media Strategy

Promotional Strategy

Market Accessibility

Business Development

STARTUP RESOURCES

Monthly Income Requirement to Support Current Lifestyle

Other Sources of Income During Startup

Savings to Support Yourself During Ramp Up

Other Investors/Partners in the Future

Loans to Support the Startup Period

Owner Investment in the Business

Financial Objective

Backup Plan

ADMINISTRATIVE RESOURCES

Registered Business Name & Tax ID

Registered Patents/Trademarks/Permits

Loans

Legal Fees

Accounting Fees

Healthcare Costs

Insurance Costs (other than healthcare)

Rent & Utility Costs

Marketing & Promotional Costs

Other Requirements

EMPLOYMENT PLAN

Number of Employees

Job Titles & Descriptions

Wages

Benefits

Other Requirements

FUTURE EXPANSION PLANS

Plans for Expanding the Current Business Model

Investment Required to Achieve Future Expansion

Business Milestones Required Before Expansion

Expansion Within the Current Business Plan

Business Sustainability

"GUT" CHECK

Have You Ever Conducted a Market Test for Your Business?

Has Anyone Tried Your Business Idea & Failed?

How is Your Business Plan Different and/or Better Than Similar Businesses?

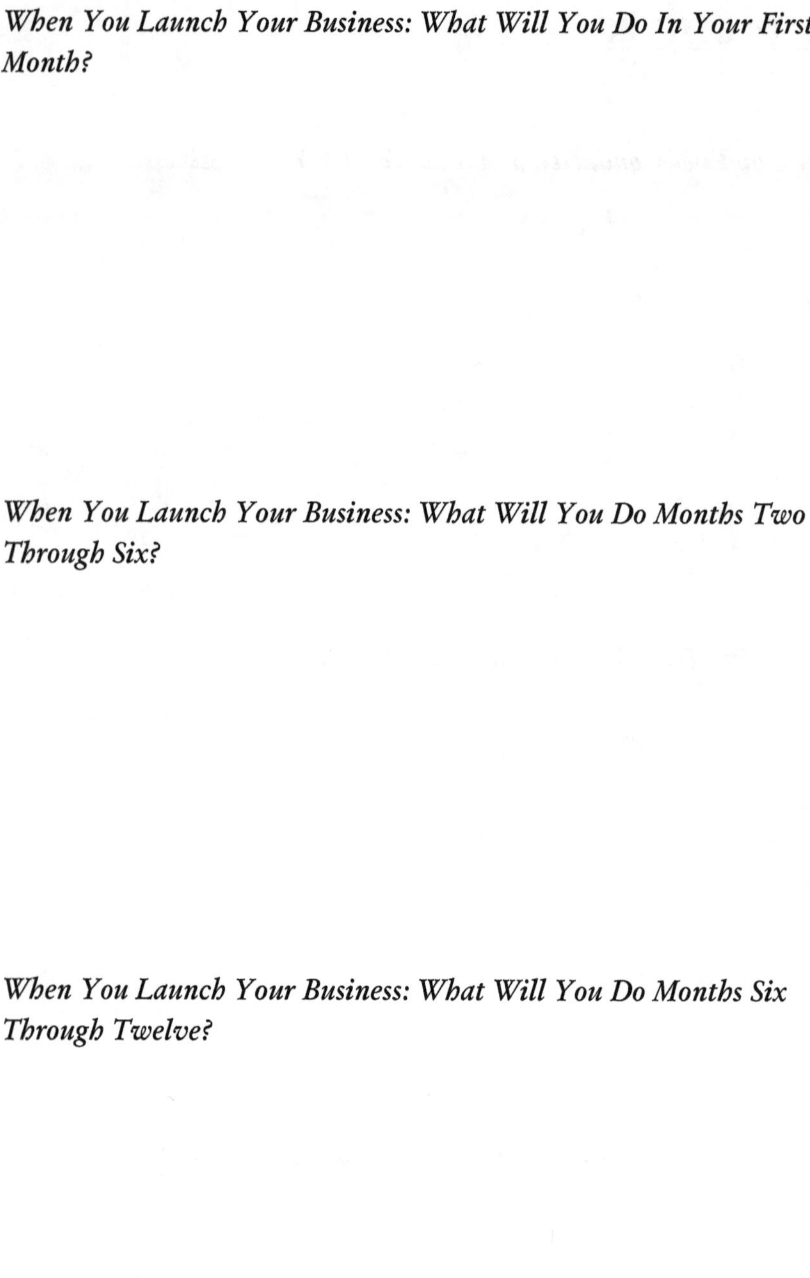

When You Launch Your Business: What Will You Do In Your First Month?

When You Launch Your Business: What Will You Do Months Two Through Six?

When You Launch Your Business: What Will You Do Months Six Through Twelve?

Where Do You Need Help?

What is Your Biggest Fear or Question Moving Forward?

INVESTMENT BREAKDOWN

What Assets Do You Need to Purchase to Get Your Business Started?

What Operating Expenses Will You Need to Pay Out-of-Pocket Until the Business Can Support Them on Its Own?

What Other Startup Expenses Will You Need to Fund?

Chart Your Investment Plan

FINANCIALS YR1

FINANCIALS YR2

FINANCIALS YR3

EXECUTIVE SUMMARY

EXECUTIVE SUMMARY

NOTES

ABOUT THE AUTHOR

Lisa Woods, President, ManagingAmericans.com
& Lisa Woods Consulting

Lisa, a thought leader in business management and leadership, founded ManagingAmericans.com in 2011 after 20+ years successfully leading and driving growth in the corporate world. Her objective is to help mentor and develop professionals to be better leaders, managers, team players and individual contributors in a "do-it-yourself" learning environment using unique & practical tools to support the process. With a B.A. in Corporate Communication and an M.B.A., Lisa's career spans from Global Sales & Marketing to General Management of multinational conglomerates. Today she continues to consult small business owners through her private practice.

Her publications include:

- 4 Essential Skills for Leaders, Managers & High Potentials © 2013
- The Cross Functional Business: Beyond Teams © 2015
- Action Item List: Drive Your Team With One Simple Tool © 2016
- Small Business Planning Made Simple: What To Consider Before You Invest © 2017

www.ingramcontent.com/pod-product-compliance
Lightning Source LLC
Chambersburg PA
CBHW051717170526
45167CB00002B/692

* 9 7 8 1 5 4 4 2 6 6 5 2 7 *